# ACKNOWLEDGEMENTS

First I would like to thank my husband, Samuel Cubbage II. Hubby, you are the one who was the guinea pig of these recipes! We had SOO much soup over the course of the Covid 19 pandemic, that I'm sure you felt as if we were going to float away! Thank you for always being my 'taste tester"! AND being willing to try the vegan versions of the soups!

Thank you to MY family; The Normans. Robert and Dorothy (Dad and Mom), and Terri (my sister). After Sam, you were also guinea pigs.. HAHA! Thank you for giving me such praise about my meals.

My in-laws and friends. By the time I got to try the recipes out on you, I had perfected them a bit. LOL! Thank YOU for eating my food; and making me think that it was good enough. HA!

# INTRODUCTION

This cookbook is an extension of the series of cookbooks that I have (am doing). Along with my cooking show "Cooking Fun with Mrs. Cubbage- The YouTube Show!" Please like, click, share and SUBSCRIBE to The CCI Radio Show Channel! There is a lot of different content there. Please, join us!

# DEDICATION

This book is dedicated to YOU! Show your love to your family and friends, by enjoying these recipes together. A high expression of love is to share your cooking with those you hold dear. That's what I did. And I hope that this cookbook will serve you well for years to come.

# TABLE OF CONTENTS

**Light Soups**
- Wedding Soup
- Kale, Sausage and Potato Soup
- Lentil Soup (vegan version available)

**Comfort Soups**
- Chicken Noodle Soup
- Vegetable Soup (Vegan version available)
- Tomato Soup (Vegan Version Available)

**Creamy Soups**
- Creamy Chicken, and Wild Rice Soup
- Creamy Potato Soup (Grown up version)
- Corn Chowder

**Dinner Soups**
- Turkey Chili
- Chicken and Dumplings
- Spiced Autumn Apple Soup (Vegan Version Available)

# Light Soups

As I was putting this book of recipes together, I found out that Wedding Soup is a Pittsburgh tradition! Living my WHOLE life in Pittsburgh, I never knew that! So, this is my version of Italian wedding soup. It's one of my favorites!!

## Homemade Italian Wedding Soup

### Ingredients:

- 1 lb box Acini de pepe pasta
- ½ pound extra-lean ground turkey (seasoned and shaped into mini-sized meatballs
- 1 egg, lightly beaten
- 2 tablespoons Italian dry bread crumbs
- 1 tablespoon fresh Parmesan cheese (heard too many things about grated parmesan that I prefer the fresh
- ½ teaspoon fresh basil
- 5 ¾ cups chicken broth
- 3 tablespoons of minced garlic
- ⅓ cup finely chopped carrot
- ½ cup of spinach

- ¼ cup of onions

## Directions:

- In a medium bowl, combine meat, egg, bread crumbs, cheese, basil and onion powder; shape into 3/4 inch balls.
- In a large saucepan, heat broth to boiling; stir in orzo pasta, chopped carrot and meatballs. Return to boil, then reduce heat to medium. Cook at slow boil for 10 minutes, or until pasta is al dente. Stir frequently to prevent sticking. Sprinkle a little parmesan cheese and enjoy!

This was a dish that I threw together...Literally! We hadn't gone to the store, had several different food items, and NO IDEA of what to do. I pulled out kale, turkey sausage and potatoes....And the rest is.... YUMMY!

# Kale, Sausage and Potato Soup

Ingredients:

1 ½ pound bulk Italian sausage (Chopped)

3 cups heavy whipping cream

3 cups cubed potatoes

2 cups low-sodium chicken broth

1 ½ cups of milk

2 ½ cups of kale leaves (chopped)

1 yellow onion, chopped

½ teaspoon italian seasonings

½ teaspoon ground black pepper

## Directions

Heat a large soup pot over medium-high heat. Place chopped sausage into the pot; cook and stir until browned, about 15 minutes. Drain and pour out the grease. (It wouldn't hurt to also pat it dry for extra grease.)

Slowly stir in heavy whipping cream, cubed potatoes, chicken broth, milk, onion, Italian seasoning into sausage. Bring mixture to a boil, and reduce heat to low. Simmer until potatoes are tender, about 35 minutes. Add black pepper; stir kale into soup. Simmer until the kale is tender, 20 more minutes. Serve hot!

# Lentil Soup

Ingredients:

1 pat of unsalted butter
1 small white onion (chopped)
1 clove of garlic
1 fresh carrot (chopped)
1 fresh stalk of celery (chopped)
1 teaspoon of Cumin
1 teaspoon of Paprika
2 cups of Lentils
2 medium tomatoes
2 cups of chicken broth
1 cup of water
2 Bay leaves
1 teaspoon of lemon juice
Salt and pepper to taste


Directions:

In a skillet, sauté your onion, garlic, carrots and celery over low heat for about 10 minutes. In a large soup pot, add the chicken broth and water. Add all above ingredients and the lentils to the large soup pot; simmer for 45 minutes (until lentils are soft); and then, add a squirt of lemon. Add salt and pepper to taste.

*NOTE TO CHEF: If you are vegan, you can make this yummy soup! Substitute the butter for olive oil. And substitute chicken broth for vegetable broth. That's it! Vegan Vegetable Soup!*

# Comfort Soups

# Chicken Noodle (or Rice) Soup

Ingredients:

- ¼ cup unsalted butter
- 1 large yellow onion, chopped
- 3 large carrots, sliced
- 3 stalks celery, sliced
- season salt, to taste
- black pepper, to taste
- 3 cloves garlic, chopped
- 8 cups chicken or vegetable broth
- 8 oz egg noodles (Or you can use rice instead)
- 5 cups chicken breast, cubed
- ¼ cup fresh parsley, chopped

Directions:

1. Melt the butter in a skillet until melted over medium heat. Add the onion, carrots, celery, stirring frequently, until the vegetables are very soft, about 15 minutes. Add to a large soup pot.
2. Using the same skillet, cook the cubed chicken for about 10 minutes.
3. In a smaller skillet, saute the garlic and cook until fragrant, about 2 minutes, on low.  In a large soup pot, add the broth and bring to a boil. Then add the garlic and chicken to the pot.
4. Add the noodles (or rice) and cook for 6 minutes, then add the chicken and cook about 2 minutes more, until the noodles (or rice) are cooked through and the chicken is warmed through.
5. Season to taste with salt and pepper, then stir in the parsley.
6. Enjoy!

# Homemade Vegetable Soup

The great thing about this recipe is that you don't need EXACT measurements for it to be good! But, since this is a 'cookbook' lol! I will give some specifics to help. :-)

Ingredients:

1 yellow onion

1 small can of tomato paste

2 carrots

2 stocks of celery

1 can of diced tomatoes

2 cans of chicken or vegetable broth

1 cup of water

2 large potatoes (any kind)

1 bag of frozen peas

1 bay leaf

Directions:

Saute onions, carrots, and celery in butter and tomato paste. Pour in vegetable or chicken stock, a can of diced tomatoes, potatoes, and bay leaf.

**Simmer until the veggies are tender (about 25 minutes).**

**Add frozen peas and cook for 7 more minutes.**

**Serve hot! Enjoy!**


*NOTE TO CHEF: If you are vegan, you can make this yummy soup! Substitute the butter for olive oil. And substitute chicken broth for vegetable broth. That's it! Vegan Vegetable Soup!*

# Homemade Tomato Soup

## *Ingredients*

4 tablespoons unsalted butter

1/2 large onion, cut into large wedges

1 (28-ounce) can tomatoes, whole peeled or crushed, see notes for fresh tomatoes. Can I use fresh tomatoes? Yes. If you want to use fresh tomatoes, you will need 9-10 medium tomatoes ( about 2 pounds). You can peel them, but you can skip this part if you are using a blender.

1 1/2 cups water

1 can of low sodium chicken stock

1/2 teaspoon fine sea salt and basil, or more to taste

## *Directions*

Melt butter over medium heat in a large saucepan.

Add onion wedges, water, can of tomatoes with their juices, and 1/2 teaspoon of salt. Bring to a simmer. Cook, uncovered, for about 40 minutes. Stirring occasionally.

Blend the soup, and then season to taste. The soup doesn't need to be super smooth. Use a blender. If you use a regular blender, blend the soup in stages and do not fill the blender as much as you normally would since the soup is hot. Once the soup is blended to your liking, feel free to enjoy!

*NOTE TO CHEF: If you are vegan, you can make this yummy soup! Substitute the butter for olive oil. And substitute chicken broth for vegetable broth. That's it! Vegan Tomato Soup!*

# Creamy Soups

# Homemade Potato soup (Grown Up Version)

In my first cookbook "Cooking Fun w/ Mrs. Cubbage" I have a potato soup recipe for the kiddos. However, THIS recipe is going to be more suited to those with 'mature' tastebuds!

### Ingredients

- 7 bacon strips, diced
- 8 large potatoes (cubed)
- 1 large carrot, grated
- 1 cup chopped onion
- 2 cans (14-1/2 ounces) chicken broth
- 3 tablespoons all-purpose flour
- 3 cups milk (feel free to use whatever type of milk you like. For the children, I found that 1% milk worked well)
- 16 ounces sharp cheddar cheese
- 8 ounces of sour cream
- 1 teaspoon of salt and pepper to taste

## Directions

Peel the potatoes with a potato peeler. Then, boil a half pot of water. Place potatoes in the water and boil for about 20 minutes. While the potatoes are boiling, you can start on the other steps.

- In a large saucepan, cook bacon over medium heat until crisp, stirring occasionally; drain drippings. Then, use the drippings to saute the onions.
- Add vegetables, including potatoes, seasonings and broth; bring to a boil. Reduce heat; simmer, covered, until potatoes are tender, 10-15 minutes. Mix flour and milk until smooth; stir into soup. Bring to a boil, stirring constantly; cook and stir until

thickened, about 2 minutes. Stir in cheese until melted. Add a dollop of sour cream, crumble your bacon and enjoy!

# Homemade Corn Chowder

- 1 tablespoon butter
- 3 strips bacon
- 1/2 large yellow onion, chopped (about 3/4 cup)
- 1/3 cup diced red bell pepper
- 1/2 cup small diced carrot
- 1/2 cup small diced celery
- 3 cans of sweet corn (drained)
- 1 bay leaf
- 4 1/2 cups milk, whole or low fat
- 2 medium potatoes, peeled and diced
- 1 tablespoon season salt
- 1/2 teaspoon freshly ground black pepper
- 1 teaspoon fresh thyme leaves

## Directions:

Place butter and bacon into a large skillet. Heat on medium heat until the bacon renders its fat, 3-4 minutes. Cook the vegetables (except the corn and potatoes). Add the chopped onions, red bell pepper, carrot, and celery, lower the heat to medium low and cook until vegetables soften, about 5 minutes. Add corn to the pot. Bring to a boil and reduce heat to a bare simmer. Cover the pot and cook for 20 minutes. Make sure the heat is as low as can be; a gentle simmer. After 20 minutes, add the potatoes, salt, and thyme to the pot. Increase the heat to return the soup to a simmer, then lower the heat to maintain the simmer and cook for another 10 minutes. Serve warm. Enjoy!

# Creamy Chicken and Rice Soup

## Ingredients:

- 1/2 cup uncooked wild rice (any blend that you like will do)
- 1 small chopped yellow onion
- 1 cup diced carrots (from 2 medium)
- 1 cup diced celery (from 2 stalks)
- 7 Tbsp butter- divided
- 3 TBS of minced garlic
- 4 1/2 cups low-sodium chicken broth
- 1/4 tsp mix of dried thyme , marjoram, sage and rosemary
- Salt and ground black pepper , to taste
- 2 lbs boneless skinless chicken breasts cubed
- 1/4 cup all-purpose flour
- 1 cups milk
- 1/2 cup heavy whipping cream

## Instructions

1. Prepare rice according to directions listed on the package.
2. Halfway through the rice cooking, in a separate large pot, melt 1 Tbsp butter over medium heat. Add onion, carrots and celery and saute until slightly tender, about 4 minutes, adding in garlic during the last 30 seconds of sauteing.
3. Add chicken broth, thyme, marjoram, sage, rosemary and season with salt and black pepper to taste. Increase heat to medium-high, add chicken and bring mixture to a boil.
4. Cover pot with lid and allow mixture to boil 12 - 15 minutes, or until chicken is cooked through (rotating chicken to opposite side once during cooking for thicker chicken breasts - if they don't fully immerse in broth).
5. Remove chicken and set aside on a cutting board to cool for 5 minutes then shred into small bite size pieces. Meanwhile reduce heat to low and add cooked rice. Add shredded chicken to soup.
6. In a separate medium saucepan (I just rinsed and wiped out the rice pan), melt remaining 6 Tbsp butter over medium heat. Add flour and cook 1 ½ minutes, whisking constantly.

7. Then, while whisking vigorously, slowly pour milk into the butter/flour mixture. Cook mixture, stirring constantly until it thickens.
8. Add milk mixture to soup mixture in pot and cook about 5 minutes longer, or until soup is thickened (at this point, you can simmer the soup for a longer period of time if you want the rice to soften more, just cover with lid first and stir occasionally.
9. You can also add what's left in the remaining can of chicken broth). Stir in heavy cream and serve warm.

# Dinner Soups

# Turkey Chili

## Ingredients:

2 pats of butter
3 pounds of ground turkey
1 yellow onion
1 large can of crushed tomatoes
1 small bag of kidney beans (I'm not a fan of beans. But, these are the best to add to the chili).
1 clove of garlic (minced).
Chili powder to taste
Hot sauce to taste
Black pepper to taste

## Directions:

- Heat the butter in a large pot over medium heat. Place turkey in the pot, and cook until evenly brown. Stir in onion, and cook until tender.
Pour water into the pot. Mix in tomatoes, kidney beans, and garlic. Season chili powder, hot sauce and pepper. Bring to a boil. Reduce heat to low, cover, and simmer for 45 minutes. Serve warm. (Serve with cornbread)! Yum!

## Chicken and Dumplings

## Ingredients:

Dumplings:
- ¾ cup milk
- 4 tablespoons butter
- 2 cups all-purpose flour
- 1 tablespoon baking powder
- 1 tablespoon chopped fresh parsley
- ¾ teaspoon salt

Chicken Mixture:

- 3 cups chicken stock
- ½ cup of milk and flour mixed
- 3 medium skinless, boneless chicken breast halves
- 2 potatoes, cubed
- 1 yellow onion, diced
- 1 stick of celery, diced
- ½ cup diced carrot
- ½ (10 ounce) package frozen peas, thawed (Optional)

Directions:

Combine flour, baking powder, parsley, and salt in a bowl. Stir in milk mixture until dough forms a ball, making sure not to overmix. Cover dumpling dough and let stand for 30 minutes. In a skillet, saute chicken until it is no longer pink in the center. Combine chicken stock and cream of chicken soup in a large saucepan. Bring to a simmer over medium-high heat. Add chicken, potatoes, onion, celery, carrots, peas, thyme. Cook vegetables until they are tender, about 12 minutes. Transfer chicken to a plate to cool; transfer vegetables to a bowl, leaving stock in the pan. Discard thyme. Boil remaining stock over medium-high heat until reduced (7 minutes).

Meanwhile, pour cream into a small saucepan and heat over medium-high heat. Cook until reduced by about 7 minutes. Whisk into reduced stock. Season with salt and pepper and set aside.

Cut cooked chicken into bite-sized pieces. Stir into stock mixture and add chicken and cooked vegetables.

Bring soup to a simmer over medium heat, adding more stock if necessary. Drop dumpling dough by teaspoons into the mixture. Cover and let simmer for 7 to 8 minutes. Serve hot. Garnished with parsley and green onion.

# Spiced Autumn Apple Soup

## INGREDIENTS

1/4 cup butter (or olive oil for vegan)
1 red onion, chopped
1 carrot, peeled and diced
3 garlic cloves, minced
2 teaspoons minced ginger
2 small green apples, peeled, diced and cored
1 (14.5 oz) can diced tomatoes
1 ½ tablespoon curry powder
½ teaspoon ground cumin
1/2 teaspoon paprika
½ teaspoon ground cinnamon
¼ teaspoon freshly ground black pepper
½ teaspoon dried thyme
½ cup kidney beans (uncooked)
3 cups chicken or vegetable broth
Salt and black pepper to taste
Toasted cashews for garnish

## INSTRUCTIONS

Melt the butter in a large pot over medium-high heat. Add the onion and carrot, then sauté for 4 to 5 minutes or until the onions have softened.

Add the garlic, ginger, apples, and diced tomatoes to the pot. Sauté on medium for another 5 minutes.

Then add in all of the spices and toss to coat.

Add in the lentils and broth and let the contents come to a boil. Turn the heat down to medium-low and simmer uncovered for 30 minutes.

Puree about 75% of the ingredients using a blender; save the other portion to not be pureed. Leave some of the chunks whole to add to the consistency of the soup.

Return the soup to the pot if needed.

Taste, and add salt and black pepper as needed.

Serve topped with cashew.
Enjoy!

*NOTE TO CHEF: If you are vegan, you can make this yummy soup! Substitute the butter for olive oil. And substitute chicken broth for vegetable broth. That's it! Vegan Spiced Autumn Apple Soup!*

www.ingramcontent.com/pod-product-compliance
Lightning Source LLC
Chambersburg PA
CBHW042128100426
42812CB00017B/2650